Red **Line 6**

Vokabellernheft

Ernst Klett Verlag
Stuttgart • Leipzig

Vorwort

Dieses Vokabellernheft im Taschenformat enthält alle Wörter und Wendungen aus *Red Line* 6. Aufgrund seines praktischen Formats kannst du es überall hin mitnehmen, um deine Wörter zu lernen und zu wiederholen.
Am besten hast du beim Lernen immer einen Bleistift zur Hand. Damit markierst du Wörter und Wendungen, die dir besondere Schwierigkeiten bereiten. Diese kannst du dann in regelmäßigen Abständen immer wieder durchgehen.

Am Ende jedes *Topic* findest du zahlreiche Übungen, mit denen du das Gelernte wiederholen, ordnen und dich auf Vokabeltests vorbereiten kannst.
Nimm dir dabei pro *Topic* zunächst alle Übungen mit dem Wortschatz *Check-in* bis *Aspects* vor und dann die Übungen zu denjenigen *Options*, die du in der Schule durchgenommen hast. Im Anschluss an die *Topics* kannst du auf den Seiten 70 bis 71 spannende Rätsel zum Vokabular des gesamten Schülerbuchs *Red Line* 6 lösen.
Die Lösungen zu allen Übungen und Rätseln findest du hinten im Heft (ab Seite 72).

Viel Spaß wünscht dir dein *Red-Line*-Team!

Topic 1 A global language

Check-in

backpacker	['bækpækə]	Rucksacktourist/-in
complaint	[kəm'pleɪnt]	Beschwerde
to **request**	[rɪ'kwest]	bitten
permission (no pl.)	[pə'mɪʃn]	Erlaubnis, Genehmigung
air traffic controller	[eə,træfik kən'trəʊlə]	Fluglotse/Fluglotsin
politician	[,pɒlɪ'tɪʃn]	Politiker/-in
call center *(AE)*	['kɔ:l ,sentə]	Callcenter *(Unternehmen für telefon. Dienstl.)*
Formula One	[,fɔ:mjələ 'wʌn]	Formel Eins
order	['ɔ:də]	Bestellung
to **deal, dealt, dealt with**	['di:l, delt, delt]	sich befassen/umgehen mit

Adjectives after verbs

Meistens verwendest du ein Adjektiv nach dem Verb *to be*, wie z. B. *The party is cool*. Es gibt jedoch bestimmte Verben, auf die ein Adjektiv folgt – manche von ihnen kennst du bereits:

*This bag **looks** great. How much is it?*
*The cake **smells** fantastic. Can I have a piece, please?*
*Bollywood films have **become** popular around the world.*
*Wait until the lights **go** green!*
*I **feel** great, I'll be on holiday tomorrow.*
*His new girlfriend **seems** very nice.*
*You needn't worry, just **stay/keep** cool.*

Language 1

to **go** (+ adj.)	[gəʊ]	werden
empire	['empaɪə]	(Kaiser-)Reich, Imperium
native speaker	[,neɪtɪv 'spi:kə]	Muttersprachler/-in
Hindi	['hɪndi:]	Hindi *(indische Sprache)*

to **include** [ɪnˈkluːd]	*hier:* beifügen
explorer [ɪkˈsplɔːrə]	Forscher/-in, Forschungsreisende(r)
trader [ˈtreɪdə]	Händler/-in
nationality [ˌnæʃnˈæləti]	Nationalität, Staatsangehörigkeit
whenever [wenˈevə]	wann immer, immer, wenn
mother tongue [ˌmʌðə ˈtʌŋ]	Muttersprache
ties pl. [taɪz]	Beziehungen, Bande
former [ˈfɔːmə]	ehemalige/-r/-s, frühere/-r/-s
to **leave out** [liːvˈaʊt]	weglassen
shower [ˈʃaʊə]	*hier:* Dusche; Schauer
contact [ˈkɒntækt]	Kontakt
chat room [ˈtʃætrʊm]	Chatroom *(Internetforum)*

Language 2

to **keep** (+ adj.) [kiːp]	bleiben
to **prepare** [prɪˈpeə]	vorbereiten, *hier:* sich vorbereiten auf; zubereiten
obviously [ˈɒbviəsli]	offensichtlich
smart [smɑːt]	*hier:* schick
interviewer [ˈɪntəvjuːə]	Interviewer/-in, Befrager/-in
immediately [ɪˈmiːdiətli]	sofort, gleich
to **note down** [ˌnəʊt ˈdaʊn]	notieren, aufschreiben
likely [ˈlaɪkli]	wahrscheinlich
office junior [ˌɒfɪs ˈdʒuːniə]	Bürogehilfe/Bürogehilfin
delivery [dɪˈlɪvri]	Lieferung
to **swap** [swɒp]	tauschen
fluent [ˈfluːənt]	fließend
handball [ˈhændbɔːl]	Handball
Let's see. [lets ˈsiː]	Lass mich mal überlegen.
Let me put that differently. [ˈdɪfrntli]	Lass es mich anders ausdrücken.
Human Resources [ˌhjuːmən rɪˈzɔːsɪz]	Personalwesen
Ms [mɪz]	Frau *(Anrede)*
department [dɪˈpɑːtmənt]	Abteilung

Everyday English: A job interview

Die folgenden *phrases* helfen dir, wenn du ein Vorstellungsgespräch hast.

I'm still at school./I left school early./I did my final exams some time ago.	Ich gehe noch zur Schule./ Ich habe die Schule abgebrochen./Ich habe vor einiger Zeit meinen Abschluss gemacht.
I'm interested in the job/ placement/… because …	Ich interessiere mich für den Job/das Praktikum/… weil …
I like working outside/with computers/with people/ in a team/…	Ich arbeite gerne im Freien/ mit Computern/mit Menschen/in einem Team …
I'd like to train to be a/an …	Ich würde mich gerne als … ausbilden lassen./Ich möchte gerne eine Ausbildung machen als …
I'd like to work with animals/…	Ich arbeite gerne mit Tieren/…
My 'dream' job would be as a …	Mein Traumberuf wäre …
I'd like to work abroad/in …	Ich würde gerne im Ausland/ in/auf … arbeiten.
I'm good/not so good at …	Ich bin (nicht so) gut im Umgang mit …
My hobbies are …	Meine Hobbys sind …
How much will I be paid?	Wie hoch ist mein Lohn/ Gehalt?
When will I have to start work in the morning?	Wann beginnt morgens die Arbeit?

Aspects

professional [prəˈfeʃnl]   *hier:* professionell; Profi-
coaching [ˈkəʊtʃɪŋ]   *hier:* Training; Nachhilfe
passion [ˈpæʃn]   Passion, Leidenschaft
wish [wɪʃ]   Wunsch

sponsor ['spɒntsə]	Sponsor/-in, Förderer/Förderin
talented ['tæləntɪd]	talentiert, begabt
multi-lingual [ˌmʌlti'lɪŋgwəl]	vielsprachig
session ['seʃn]	Einheit, Sitzung, Stunde
to assess [ə'ses]	bewerten, beurteilen, einschätzen
trial ['traɪəl]	Prüfung, Test
admission [əd'mɪʃn]	*hier:* Aufnahme, Zulassung
Canadian [kə'neɪdiən]	kanadisch; Kanadier/-in
majority [mə'dʒɒrəti]	Mehrheit(en-)
Inuktitut [ɪ'nʊktɪtʊt]	Inuktitut *(Sprache der Inuit)*
Inuit ['ɪnuɪt]	Inuit *(arktisches Volk)*
non-official [ˌnɒnə'fɪʃl]	inoffiziell
Punjabi [pʌn'dʒɑːbiː]	Punjabi *(indische Sprache)*
foreign language [ˌfɒrɪn 'læŋgwɪdʒ]	Fremdsprache
pukka ['pʌkə]	echt *(ugs.)*
Hinglish ['hɪŋglɪʃ]	Hinglisch *(Mischung aus Hindi und Englisch)*
mixture ['mɪkstʃə]	Mischung, Gemisch, Mixtur
Urdu ['ʊədu:]	Urdu *(pakistanische und indische Sprache)*
subcontinent [sʌb'kɒntɪnənt]	Subkontinent
to spread, spread, spread [spred, spred, spred]	(sich) ausbreiten, (sich) verbreiten
rapid ['ræpɪd]	schnell, rasch, rapide
common ['kɒmən]	gebräuchlich, verbreitet
whom [hu:m]	*hier:* wem; wen *(formelle Sprache)*
baggage (no pl.) ['bægɪdʒ]	(Reise-)Gepäck

Option 1

webzine ['webzi:n]	Webmagazin
a couple of ['kʌpl]	einige, ein paar
hardly ['hɑːdli]	kaum

Vocabulary 1

whatever (the reason) [wɒt'evə] — was auch immer, egal was (der Grund ist)
certainly ['sɜ:tnli] — sicher, gewiss
future ['fju:tʃə] — zukünftig
participant [pɑ:'tɪsɪpənt] — Teilnehmer/-in
immersion school [ɪ'mɜ:ʃn ˌsku:l] — Schule, in der in einer Fremdspr. unterrichtet wird
sort of ['sɔ:t ˌəv] — irgendwie, ein Stück weit
bilingual [baɪ'lɪŋgwəl] — zweisprachig, bilingual
to be hopeless ['həʊpləs] — ein hoffnungsloser Fall sein
Zulu ['zu:lu:] — Zulu (südafrik. Sprache)
scholarship ['skɒləʃɪp] — Stipendium
to manage to (do s.th.) ['mænɪdʒ] — schaffen (etw. zu tun); hier: zurechtkommen
offside [ˌɒf'saɪd] — Abseits
header ['hedə] — Kopfball
Cantonese [ˌkæntə'ni:z] — Kantonesisch (mit dem Chinesischen verwandte Sprache); Kantonese/Kantonesin

podcast ['pɒdkɑ:st] — Podcast
to label ['leɪbl] — beschriften, benennen, etikettieren

Option 2

secondary school ['sekəndri ˌsku:l] — weiterführende Schule

talent ['tælənt] — Talent
I don't mind. [maɪnd] — Ich habe nichts dagegen., Es ist mir egal.

to emigrate ['emɪgreɪt] — emigrieren, auswandern
elementary school (AE) [elɪ'mentri ˌsku:l] — Grundschule
junior high school (AE) [ˌdʒu:niə 'haɪ ˌsku:l] — Junior High School (Vorstufe zur High School, meist 7.–9. Klasse)

manga ['mæŋgə] — Manga (japan. Comicform)

1 Vocabulary

storyboard [ˈstɔːribɔːd]	Storyboard *(gezeichnete Version eines Drehbuchs)*
animé [ˈænɪmeɪ]	animierter Manga
forum [ˈfɔːrəm]	Forum
instruction book [ɪnˈstrʌkʃn ˌbʊk]	Handbuch
to **set, set, set up** [set, set, set]	gründen, aufbauen
to **scan** [skæn]	(ein)scannen
link [lɪŋk]	Link, Verbindung
amazed [əˈmeɪzd]	erstaunt, verblüfft
technique [tekˈniːk]	Methode, Technik
review [rɪˈvjuː]	Kritik, Rezension
final [ˈfaɪnl]	letzte/-r/-s
to **influence** [ˈɪnfluənts]	beeinflussen
Western [ˈwestən]	westlich
must [mʌst]	Muss
lover [ˈlʌvə]	Liebhaber/-in; Geliebte(r)
even if [ˌiːvnˈɪf]	auch wenn

Option 3

close [kləʊs]	genau
to **overhear** [ˌəʊvəˈhɪə]	zufällig mitanhören, belauschen
fusion [ˈfjuːʒn]	Fusion, Verbindung, Verschmelzung
exaggerated [ɪgˈzæʤreɪtɪd]	übertrieben
unlike [ʌnˈlaɪk]	anders als, im Gegensatz zu
couch potato [ˈkaʊtʃ pəˌteɪtəʊ]	Couchpotato, Fernsehglotzer/-in *(ugs.)*
expression [ɪkˈspreʃn]	Ausdruck, Redewendung
clearly [ˈklɪəli]	eindeutig, offensichtlich
to **exist** [ɪgˈzɪst]	existieren
doubleclick [ˈdʌblklɪk]	Doppelklick
term [tɜːm]	*hier:* Begriff
to **replace** [rɪˈpleɪs]	ersetzen

screenager ['skri:neɪdʒə]	Bildschirm-Teenie *(ugs.)*
influence ['ɪnfluənts]	Einfluss
lifestyle ['laɪfstaɪl]	Lebensart
homie ['həʊmi]	Kumpel *(ugs.)*
hood [hʊd]	Nachbarschaft *(ugs.)*
religious [rɪ'lɪdʒəs]	religiös
assassin [ə'sæsɪn]	Mörder/-in
among [ə'mʌŋ]	unter (zwischen)
bit [bɪt]	Stückchen; *hier:* Auszug, Teil
cultural ['kʌltʃrl]	kulturell
culture ['kʌltʃə]	Kultur
to **catch** [kætʃ]	hören, aufschnappen
to **serve** [sɜ:v]	servieren
pot [pɒt]	Topf
spice [spaɪs]	Gewürz
metal ['metl]	(aus) Metall
to **translate** [trænz'leɪt]	übersetzen
vegetarian [ˌvedʒɪ'teəriən]	Vegetarier/-in
hot [hɒt]	*hier:* scharf
collage [kɒl'ɑ:ʒ]	Collage
to **search** [sɜ:tʃ]	(durch)suchen

Weitere Mengenangaben

Viele englische Substantive haben – zum Teil anders als im Deutschen – keine Pluralform. Man sagt einfach *some information/news/advice* usw. Um zum Beispiel über eine bestimmte Information zu sprechen, muss man eine dieser Umschreibungen verwenden:

a piece of information – eine Information
a bit of news – eine (kleine) Nachricht
an item of furniture – ein Möbelstück
a good piece of advice – ein guter Ratschlag

Solche Wörter sind in Wörterbüchern mit dem Verweis „kein Plural" oder „nicht zählbar" gekennzeichnet.

Exercises

Exercises with words from Check-in to Aspects

1 Languages

Unterstreiche die Wörter, die etwas mit Sprachen zu tun haben.

native speaker	nationality	order	Hindi
department	mother tongue	wish	sponsor
fluent	handball	trial	rapid
multi-lingual	common	Punjabi	Urdu
mixture	majority	German	spoken
translation	likely	country	words

2 Almost the same!

Notiere die englischen Übersetzungen. Achte dabei auf die kleinen Unterschiede in der Schreibung.

1. Politiker / -in = _____

2. Callcenter = _____

3. Nationalität = _____

4. Kontakt = _____

5. Chatroom = _____

6. Interviewer / -in = _____

7. notieren = _____

8. Handball = _____

9. professionell = _____

10. Passion = _____

3 Hyphen or no hyphen?

Kombiniere jeweils zwei Wörter, um einen neuen Ausdruck zu erhalten. Schreibe diesen dann in die richtige Gruppe.

sub	center	multi	mother	official	tongue
made	full	continent	speaker	lingual	call
native	non	home	time		

with hyphen **without hyphen**

_____ _____

_____ _____

_____ _____

_____

4 Which word?

Welches Wort wird hier gesucht?

1. The language of the Inuits: _____

2. A tourist with a rucksack: _____

3. Britain had this until 1945: _____

4. How you should dress for an interview: _____

5. It's quicker than taking a bath: _____

6. If you can speak a language well, you are _____.

7. There are many of these in a company: _____

Exercises

5 New words

Welche Wörter aus Topic 1 kannst du von diesen Wörtern ableiten?

1. coach → _____

2. talent → _____

3. bag → _____

4. to complain → _____

5. interview → _____

6. to deliver → _____

7. national → _____

6 Definitions

Erkläre diese vier Begriffe auf Englisch.

1. multi-lingual _____
_____

2. sponsor _____
_____

3. Hinglish _____
_____

4. common _____
_____

7 Opposites

a) *Wie lautet das Gegenteil?*

1. official → _____

2. mother tongue → _____

3. interviewee → _____

4. later → _____

b) *Die folgenden Vorsilben verändern die Bedeutung eines Wortes (häufig hin zum Gegenteil). Schreibe zu jeder Vorsilbe ein Beispielwort auf.*

1. dis- → _____

2. im- → _____

3. ir- → _____

4. un- → _____

8 What's the word?

Wie heißen diese Wörter auf Englisch?

1. Erlaubnis _____

2. Einheit, Sitzung _____

3. Leidenschaft _____

4. (sich) ausbreiten _____

5. vielsprachig _____

6. Mehrheit _____

1 Exercises

9 Word lines

Welches Wort aus Topic 1 passt ...

a) *... inhaltlich in die jeweilige Reihe?*

1. Hindi, Urdu, _____

2. thief, criminal, _____

3. to interview, interviewee, _____

4. sink, bath, _____

b) *... der Endung nach in die jeweilige Reihe?*

1. pass**ion**, sess**ion**, _____

2. backpack**er**, tow**er**, _____

3. entertain**ment**, com**ment**, _____

4. lugg**age**, teen**age**, _____

10 Matching verbs

Ordne die englischen Verben den deutschen Übersetzungen zu.

1. to swap
2. to keep
3. to request
4. to deal with
5. to spread
6. to assess
7. to include
8. to prepare

a) bewerten
b) beifügen
c) sich befassen mit
d) bleiben
e) sich vorbereiten
f) tauschen
g) (sich) ausbreiten
h) bitten

11 What do you say?

Übersetze diese Sätze ins Englische.

1. Früher sprach ich nur meine Muttersprache, Inuktitut.

   _____

   _____

2. Ich arbeite für eine Firma, die sich schnell ausgebreitet

   hat. _____

   _____

3. Mein Traumberuf wäre Forscher. _____

   _____

4. Kannst du dich bitte beschreiben? _____

   _____

5. Ich arbeite gerne mit meinen Händen. _____

   _____

6. Meine Hobbys sind Radfahren und Schwimmen. _____

   _____

7. Ich habe letztes Jahr meinen Abschluss gemacht. ____

   _____

1 Exercises

Exercises for Option 1

12 Odd one out

a) *Welches Wort passt nicht in die jeweilige Gruppe? Unterstreiche es.*

_____	_____	_____
foul	bilingual	Zulu
offside	webzine	Cape Town
header	future	Cantonese
whatever	hopeless	Urdu

_____	_____
explorer	immersion
trader	high
former	university
participant	primary

b) *Füge zu jeder Gruppe einen Titel hinzu.*

13 Endings

Welche Wörter in Option 1 haben diese Endungen? Schreibe sie zusammen mit einem weiteren Beispiel auf.

1. -ese: _____

   _____

2. -ship: _____

   _____

3. -ual: _____

   _____

4. -less: _____

   _____

Exercises for Option 2

14 Sounds

Schreibe die Wörter auf, die sich hinter der Lautschrift verbergen, und übersetze sie dann ins Deutsche.

1. ['sekəndri ˌskuːl] _____

   _____

2. ['stɔːribɔːd] _____

3. [rɪ'vjuː] _____

4. ['emɪgreɪt] _____

15 Which word?

Wähle das richtige Wort, um die Sätze zu ergänzen.

1. Before you produce a comic you have to draw a _____.
   Western   technique   storyboard   3D

2. Japanese-style pictures are called _____.
   talents   lovers   amazed   mangas

3. Primary school is the same as _____ school.
   high   elementary   secondary   junior high

4. He is good at drawing. I think he has a real _____.
   must   forum   talent   lover

Exercises

Exercise for Option 3

16 Word groups

Sortiere diese Wörter in die jeweils richtige Gruppe.

exaggerated   bit   hood   screenager   among
catch   collage   search   exist   homie

1. _____
   young person
   teenager
   kid

2. _____
   beside
   around
   between

3. _____
   overdone
   made up
   said it was better

4. _____
   area
   neighborhood
   quarter

5. _____
   piece
   part
   share

6. _____
   be
   live
   be alive

7. _____
   hear
   listen
   overhear

8. _____
   friend
   mate
   guys

9. _____
   picture
   poster
   painting

10. _____
    look for
    scan
    look everywhere

Exercise for all of Topic 1

17 Personal qualities

a) Schreibe sechs Wörter aus Topic 1 auf, die du benutzen würdest, um dich selbst zu beschreiben.

1. _____   4. _____

2. _____   5. _____

3. _____   6. _____

b) Bilde mit den Wörtern aus Teil a) je einen Satz über dich.

1. _____
   _____

2. _____
   _____

3. _____
   _____

4. _____
   _____

5. _____
   _____

6. _____
   _____

Topic 2 Change it!

Check-in

politics ['pɒlɪtɪks]	Politik
to **have s.th. in common** [ˌhæv ɪn 'kɒmən]	etw. gemeinsam haben
politician [ˌpɒlɪ'tɪʃn]	Politiker/-in
campaign [kæm'peɪn]	Kampagne; Aktion
peaceful ['piːsfl]	friedlich
demonstration [ˌdemən'streɪʃn]	Demonstration
power station ['paʊə ˌsteɪʃn]	Kraftwerk
delivery [dɪ'lɪvri]	Lieferung
demonstrator ['demənstreɪtə]	Demonstrant/-in
to **lie, lay, lain** [laɪ, leɪ, leɪn]	liegen
tear gas ['tɪə ˌgæs]	Tränengas
to **demonstrate** ['demənstreɪt]	demonstrieren
troops pl. [truːps]	Truppen, Soldaten
voting station [ˌvəʊtɪŋ 'steɪʃn]	Wahllokal
turnout ['tɜːnaʊt]	Wahlbeteiligung
candidate ['kændɪdət]	Kandidat/-in

Language

valid ['vælɪd]	gültig, rechtskräftig
court [kɔːt]	Gericht
no longer [nəʊ 'lɒŋgə]	nicht mehr, nicht länger
pub [pʌb]	Kneipe; Gasthaus
illegal [ɪ'liːgl]	illegal; rechtswidrig
to **break up s.th.** [breɪk 'ʌp]	etw. beenden, auflösen
countryside ['kʌntrɪsaɪd]	Land(schaft)
to **hide s.th.** [haɪd]	etw. verbergen, verheimlichen
replacement [rɪ'pleɪsmənt]	Ersatz
I don't mean to be rude ... [miːn]	Ich möchte nicht unhöflich sein ...
to **get on s.o.'s nerves** [nɜːvz]	jdm. auf die Nerven gehen

Everyday English: Talking about society

Die folgenden *phrases* können dir helfen, wenn du ein Gespräch zum Thema *society* führst

I think our government ...	Ich denke, dass unsere Regierung ...
I'm glad we don't have ... in our country.	Ich bin froh, dass es in unserem Land keine ... gibt.
I think that young people should ...	Ich denke, junge Leute sollten ...
If I was in the government, I would fight for ... / change ...	Wenn ich an der Regierung wäre, würde ich für ... kämpfen / ... verändern.
I think the biggest problems in our society today are ... and ...	Meiner Meinung nach sind die Hauptprobleme in der heutigen Gesellschaft ... und ...
I think everyone in our society should vote / feel responsible for / ...	Ich finde, dass jedes Mitglied unserer Gesellschaft zur Wahl gehen sollte / sich verantwortlich für ... fühlen sollte / ...

to **disturb** [dɪ'stɜːb]	stören
chat room ['tʃætrʊm]	Chatroom *(Internetforum)*
motorway *(BE)* ['məʊtəweɪ]	Autobahn

Aspects

democracy [dɪ'mɒkrəsi]	Demokratie
democratic [ˌdemə'krætɪk]	demokratisch
head of state [ˌhed əv 'steɪt]	Staatsoberhaupt
monarch ['mɒnək]	Monarch/-in
previous ['priːviəs]	vorherig, vorausgegangen
head of government [ˌhed əv 'gʌvənmənt]	Regierungschef/-in
prime minister [ˌpraɪm 'mɪnɪstə]	Premierminister/-in, Ministerpräsident/-in

2 Vocabulary

minister [ˈmɪnɪstə]	Minister/-in
Congress [ˈkɒŋgres]	Kongress *(Parlament der USA)*
the **Senate** [ˈsenɪt]	der Senat *(US-amerik. Oberhaus)*
the **House of Representatives** [ˌhaʊs əv reprɪˈzentətɪvz]	das US-amerik. Unterhaus
representative [ˌreprɪˈzentətɪv]	Vertreter/-in, Abgeordnete(r), Repräsentant/-in
the **House of Commons** [ˌhaʊs əv ˈkɒmənz]	das britische Unterhaus
MP (= **Member of Parliament**) [ˌemˈpiː]	Mitglied des brit. Parlaments
the **House of Lords** [ˌhaʊs əv ˈlɔːdz]	das britische Oberhaus
every [ˈevri]	alle
senator [ˈsenətə]	Senator/-in
among others [əˌmʌŋ ˈʌðəz]	unter anderen
column [ˈkɒləm]	Spalte
hoodie [ˈhʊdi]	Kapuzenjacke/-shirt
to **launch** [lɔːnʃ]	*hier:* starten
goodie [ˈgʊdi]	guter Mensch *(ugs.)*
such as [ˈsʌtʃ əz]	wie (zum Beispiel)
anti-social [ˌæntɪˈsəʊʃl]	unsozial
stereotype [ˈsteriəʊtaɪp]	Stereotyp, Klischee
need [niːd]	Bedürfnis
message [ˈmesɪdʒ]	*hier:* Botschaft

Option 1

daily [ˈdeɪli]	täglich
monarchy [ˈmɒnəki]	Monarchie
political [pəˈlɪtɪkl]	politisch
to **wake s.o. (up)** [ˌweɪk ˈʌp]	jdn. (auf)wecken
chambermaid [ˈtʃeɪmbəmeɪd]	Zimmermädchen
matter [ˈmætə]	Angelegenheit; Frage
husband [ˈhʌzbənd]	Ehemann
ambassador [æmˈbæsədə]	Botschafter/-in

Vocabulary 2

throne [θrəʊn]	Thron
honour ['ɒnə]	Auszeichnung
corridor ['kɒrɪdɔː]	Gang, Flur, Korridor
in full regalia [ɪn ˌfʊl rɪˈɡeɪliə]	in voller Montur *(als Königin mit allen Insignien)*
occasionally [əˈkeɪʒnli]	gelegentlich
executive [ɪɡˈzekjətɪv]	Direktor/-in, Geschäftsführer/-in
to **join** [ʤɔɪn]	*hier:* sich dazugesellen
likely ['laɪkli]	wahrscheinlich
to **devote** [dɪˈvəʊt]	widmen; verwenden
social ['səʊʃl]	sozial, *hier:* gesellschaftlich
patron ['peɪtrn]	Schirmherr/-in
to **be present** [bi 'preznt]	anwesend/zugegen sein
quarters pl. ['kwɔːtəz]	Wohnung, Gemächer *(im Schloss)*
crossword ['krɒswɜːd]	Kreuzworträtsel
tray [treɪ]	Tablett
to **study** ['stʌdi]	studieren, *hier:* eingehend betrachten; lernen
confidential [ˌkɒnfɪˈdenʃl]	vertraulich
no matter (what/when/where ...) [nəʊ ˈmætə]	egal (was / wann / wo ...)
to **dislike** [dɪsˈlaɪk]	nicht mögen
to **crown** [kraʊn]	krönen
Ma'am [mɑːm]	gnädige Frau

Option 2

aim [eɪm]	Ziel, Absicht
undervalued [ˌʌndəˈvæljuːd]	unterbewertet, unterschätzt
to **misrepresent** [ˌmɪsreprɪˈzent]	falsch darstellen
to **be based on** [biː ˈbeɪst ɒn]	basieren auf, sich stützen auf
aged [eɪʤd]	im Alter von
to **emerge** [ɪˈmɜːʤ]	sich herausstellen, herauskommen
majority [məˈʤɒrəti]	Mehrheit(en-)

to **represent** [ˌreprɪˈzent]	repräsentieren; darstellen
to **portray** [pɔːˈtreɪ]	porträtieren, darstellen
to **lead, led, led** [liːd, led, led]	führen
to **hang around** [ˌhæŋ‿əˈraʊnd]	herumhängen
to **aim** [eɪm]	beabsichtigen, zielen auf, sich richten an
view [vjuː]	*hier:* Ansicht, Einstellung; Standpunkt
generation [ˌdʒenəˈreɪʃn]	Generation
constructive [kənˈstrʌktɪv]	konstruktiv
to **undermine** [ˌʌndəˈmaɪn]	schwächen, untergraben
key player [ˌkiː ˈpleɪə]	Schlüsselfigur
to **comment** [ˈkɒment]	kommentieren
to **stab** [stæb]	(mit dem Messer) stechen
rescue [ˈreskjuː]	Rettung
to **face** [feɪs]	sich einer Sache stellen
Xmas (= Christmas) [ˈkrɪsməs]	Weihnachten
jail [dʒeɪl]	Gefängnis
drunken [ˈdrʌŋkən]	betrunken
pensioner [ˈpenʃnə]	Rentner/-in
AIDS [eɪdz]	AIDS *(erworbene Immunabwehrschwäche)*
to **appear** [əˈpɪə]	auftreten; *hier:* erscheinen
to **speculate** [ˈspekjəleɪt]	spekulieren, vermuten
collage [kɒˈlɑːʒ]	Collage

Option 3

tragedy [ˈtrædʒədi]	Tragödie
lately [ˈleɪtli]	in letzter Zeit, kürzlich
to **rest in peace** [rest ɪn ˈpiːs]	in Frieden ruhen
period *(AE)* [ˈpɪəriəd]	Punkt (aus)
cop *(AE)* [kɒp]	Polizist/-in *(ugs.)*
hot [hɒt]	*hier:* erregt *(ugs.)*
on the block [blɒk]	in der Gegend *(ugs.)*
to **make bail** [meɪk ˈbeɪl]	Kaution stellen
spirits pl. [ˈspɪrɪts]	Stimmung
pain [peɪn]	Schmerz
innocent [ˈɪnəsnt]	unschuldig

The media

Diese Wörter sind recht nützlich, wenn du über Medien sprechen möchtest:

blog	Blog, Internettagebuch
blogosphere ['blɒgəsfɪə]	Blogwelt
daily newspaper	Tageszeitung
editor	Redakteur / -in
editorial [ˌedɪ'tɔːriəl]	Leitartikel
feature	*hier:* Sonderbeitrag
gossip column	Klatschspalte
headline	Schlagzeile
journalist	Journalist / -in
lead story	Aufmacher
Letters to the Editor	Leserbriefe
local paper	Lokalblatt
magazine	Zeitschrift
the media	die Medien
the news	die Nachrichten
newspaper	Zeitung
the press	die Presse
report	Bericht
reporter	Reporter / -in

sniper ['snaɪpə]	Scharfschütze, Heckenschütze
though [ðəʊ]	obwohl
to **devastate** ['devəsteɪt]	zerstören, verwüsten
to **motivate** ['məʊtɪveɪt]	motivieren, anspornen
to **pray** [preɪ]	beten
faith [feɪθ]	Vertrauen; *hier:* Glaube *(religiös)*
the **Lord** [lɔːd]	der Herr (Gott)
forward ['fɔːwəd]	vorwärts
prayer [preə]	Gebet
hopeful ['həʊpfl]	zuversichtlich
grown [ɡrəʊn]	erwachsen, ausgewachsen

Vocabulary

Verbs with prefixes

Du kannst auch Vorsilben *(prefixes)* an Verben hängen, um neue Verben zu bilden.

Die Vorsilbe *dis-* gibt dem Verb eine gegenteilige Bedeutung:

→ to **dis**like nicht mögen
→ to **dis**appear verschwinden
→ to **dis**agree nicht zustimmen, nicht einverstanden sein

Die Vorsilbe *mis-* zeigt, dass etwas schlecht oder falsch gemacht wird:

→ to **mis**represent falsch darstellen
→ to **mis**read falsch lesen; falsch verstehen
→ to **mis**count sich verzählen, sich verrechnen

Die Vorsilbe *un-* kennst du bereits von Adjektiven wie *unhappy* und *uncool*. Sie wird auch mit einigen Verben verwendet:

→ to **un**do öffnen, aufmachen
→ to **un**lock aufschließen

---

to **lack** [læk] etw. nicht haben
to **keep** (+ doing) [ki:p] etwas weiter/immer wieder tun

to **achieve** [ə'tʃi:v] erringen; leisten; vollbringen
wonder ['wʌndə] Wunder
vision ['vɪʒn] Vision, Vorstellung
heat [hi:t] Hitze; *hier:* Erregung
bullet ['bʊlɪt] Kugel
to **maintain** [meɪn'teɪn] beibehalten, bleiben, *hier:* aufrecht bleiben; etw. instand halten

chorus ['kɔ:rəs] Refrain
pre-chorus [ˌpri:'kɔ:rəs] Vorrefrain
wish [wɪʃ] Wunsch
mustard seed ['mʌstəd ˌsi:d] Senfkorn

Check-out

seat belt ['siːt ˌbelt]   Sicherheitsgurt
cloudy ['klaʊdi]   wolkig
to list [lɪst]   auflisten

Exercises with words from Check-in to Aspects

1 Matching verbs

Ordne jedes Verb einer deutschen Übersetzung zu.

1. to disturb
2. to lie
3. to have s.th. in common
4. to get on s.o.'s nerves
5. to launch

a) liegen
b) jdm. auf die Nerven gehen
c) starten
d) stören
e) etw. gemeinsam haben

2 GB or USA?

Schreibe die Wörter in die jeweils richtige Gruppe. Achtung: Ein Wort passt in beide Gruppen!

House of Lords   prime minister   the Senate   president   candidate   House of Representatives   senator   Congress   House of Commons   monarch   queen/king

Great Britain   **United States of America**

_____   _____

_____   _____

_____   _____

_____   _____

_____   _____

_____   _____

2 Exercises

3 Matching words

Welche Wörter passen zusammen? Verbinde die richtigen Wörter und verwende dabei 'of', wenn nötig.

head		others
no		room
chat		Parliament
among	of	station
voting		state
Member		longer
motor		government
head		way

4 One word, two meanings

Welches englische Wort hat die jeweiligen zwei Bedeutungen?

1. gültig, rechtskräftig _____

2. Kneipe; Gasthaus _____

3. etw. beenden, auflösen _____

4. vorherig, vorausgegangen _____

5. Vertreter / -in, Abgeordnete(r) _____

6. Botschaft; Nachricht _____

7. etw. verbergen, verheimlichen _____

5 Definitions

Erkläre diese vier Begriffe auf Englisch.

1. countryside _____

   _____

2. campaign _____

   _____

3. delivery _____

   _____

4. turnout _____

   _____

6 The correct meaning

Was bedeuten diese Wörter?

1. candidate
   a) someone who wants to be voted for
   b) someone who votes

2. illegal
   a) against the rules
   b) not in the rules

3. turnout
   a) the wrong way round
   b) the number of people who vote

4. chat room
   a) a place on the Internet you can talk in
   b) another word for office

5. previous
   a) the one after
   b) the one before

6. goodie
   a) a good person
   b) a type of sweet

2 Exercises

7 Word lines

Welches Wort aus Topic 2 passt …

a) *… inhaltlich in die jeweilige Reihe?*

1. road, street, _____

2. café, restaurant, _____

3. letter, e-mail, _____

b) *… der Endung nach in die jeweilige Reihe?*

1. power**ful**, care**ful**, _____

2. stat**ion**, revis**ion**, _____

3. musi**cian**, Russ**ian**, _____

4. conditiona**l**, festiva**l**, _____

5. apart**ment**, docu**ment**, _____

6. supervis**or**, act**or**, _____

8 Sounds

Übertrage diese Wörter aus der Lautschrift.

1. [ˌpɒlɪˈtɪʃn] _____   6. [ˈtɪə ˌgæs] _____

2. [ˈkændɪdət] _____   7. [kɔːt] _____

3. [pʌb] _____   8. [ˈvælɪd] _____

4. [truːps] _____   9. [dɪˈstɜːb] _____

5. [ˈmɪnɪstə] _____   10. [ˈhʊdi] _____

30

9 What do you say?

Wie heißen diese Sätze auf Englisch? Übersetze sie.

1. Ich denke, dass unsere Regierung gut ist.

    _____

2. Ich finde, dass jedes Mitglied unserer Gesellschaft zur Wahl gehen soll. _____

    _____

3. Ich finde, dass sich junge Leute für die Umwelt verantwortlich fühlen sollten. _____

    _____

4. Meiner Meinung nach ist das Hauptproblem die Umweltverschmutzung. _____

    _____

5. Ich bin froh, dass es in unserem Land keinen Krieg gibt.

    _____

    _____

6. Wenn ich an der Regierung wäre, würde ich für mehr Schulen kämpfen. _____

    _____

Exercise for Option 1

10 Word puzzle

Finde die folgenden Wörter, die sich senkrecht, waagerecht und diagonal im Gitternetz verstecken.

ambassador	chambermaid	confidential	corridor
crossword	honour	husband	join
likely	matter	monarchy	occasionally
patron	political	social	throne
tray	wake		

C	O	N	F	I	D	E	N	T	I	A	L
R	H	C	O	R	R	I	D	O	R	T	H
O	E	A	P	M	O	N	A	R	C	H	Y
S	P	A	M	B	A	S	S	A	D	O	R
S	H	O	P	B	R	T	O	J	O	I	N
W	U	T	L	A	E	H	T	C	E	S	I
O	S	H	I	I	T	R	O	E	I	D	E
R	B	R	K	W	T	R	M	N	R	A	N
D	A	O	E	A	R	I	O	A	O	T	L
O	N	N	L	K	A	F	C	N	I	U	T
H	D	E	Y	E	Y	E	U	A	S	D	R
O	C	C	A	S	I	O	N	A	L	L	Y

Die Buchstaben, die übrig bleiben, ergeben den Titel einer sehr wichtigen Person:

_____

_____

Exercise for Option 2

11 Verbs, verbs, verbs

Wie heißen diese Verben auf Englisch?

1. vermuten = to _____

2. sich einer Sache stellen = to _____

3. stechen = to _____

4. erscheinen = to _____

5. falsch darstellen = to _____

6. schwächen = to _____

7. sich herausstellen = to _____

8. kommentieren = to _____

9. sich stützen auf = to be _____

10. porträtieren = to _____

11. führen = to _____

12. zielen auf = to _____

13. herumhängen = to _____

14. darstellen = to _____

Exercise for Option 3

12 Word puzzle

Welches Wort versteckt sich hier? Benutze die Hinweise.

1. The direction in which you walk or drive most of the time.
2. An amazing or surprising event.
3. When someone encourages you to do something.
4. This part of a song is sung more than once.
5. The American word for what you put at the end of a sentence when you write.
6. What you shoot from a gun.
7. Not a long time ago, but in the last few weeks.
8. This is a picture you see in your head.
9. The opposite of guilty.
10. When you don't have something.

Now think of a clue for number 11: _____

_____

34

Exercise for all of Topic 2

13 Word circle

Übersetze die deutschen Wörter aus Topic 2 und trage sie in den Kreis ein. Der letzte Buchstabe eines Lösungswortes ist gleichzeitig der erste Buchstabe des nächsten Wortes.

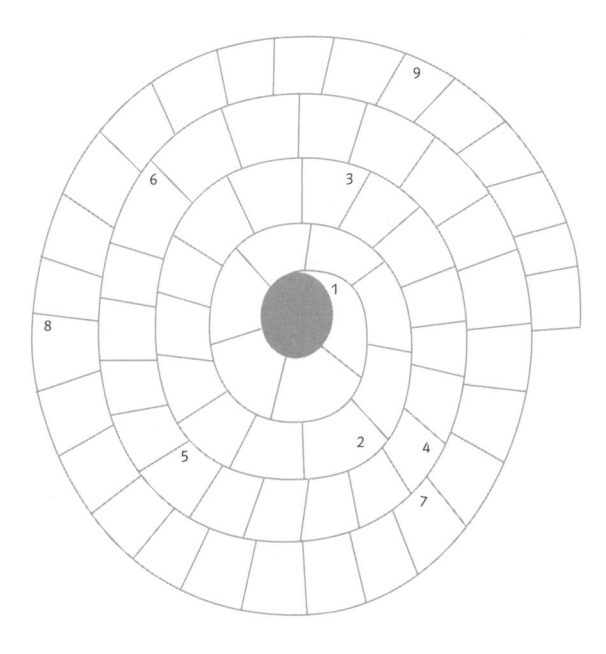

1. Rentner / -in
2. repräsentieren
3. Wahlbeteiligung
4. obwohl
5. Auszeichnung
6. Ersatz (pl.)
7. Stereotyp
8. Direktoren
9. Scharfschütze

Topic 3 This is India!

Check-in

densely populated [ˌdensli 'pɒpjəleɪtɪd]	dicht bevölkert
rural ['rʊərl]	ländlich
area ['eəriə]	*hier:* Fläche
formerly ['fɔːməli]	früher, ehemals
clothing ['kləʊðɪŋ]	Kleidung
textiles pl. ['tekstaɪlz]	Textilien, Textilware
engineering [ˌendʒɪ'nɪərɪŋ]	Ingenieurwissenschaft, Technik
software ['sɒftweə]	Software
average ['ævrɪdʒ]	durchschnittlich, Durchschnitts-
income ['ɪnkʌm]	Einkommen
currency ['kʌrntsi]	Währung
rupee [ruː'piː]	Rupie
Hindu ['hɪnduː]	Hindu; hinduistisch
Muslim ['mʊzlɪm]	Moslem/-in; Muslim/-in; moslemisch; muslimisch
religious [rɪ'lɪdʒəs]	religiös
Christian ['krɪstʃən]	Christ/-in
rickshaw ['rɪkʃɔː]	Rikscha *(Fahrradtaxi)*
crowded ['kraʊdɪd]	überfüllt
ox [ɒks] pl. **oxen** ['ɒksn]	Ochse(n)
Hindi ['hɪndiː]	Hindi *(indische Sprache)*
tie [taɪ]	Krawatte
hot [hɒt]	*hier:* scharf
dish [dɪʃ]	Gericht, Speise
vegetarian [ˌvedʒɪ'teəriən]	Vegetarier/-in

Language 1

port [pɔːt]	Hafen(stadt)
major ['meɪdʒə]	Haupt-; wichtig; groß
financial [faɪ'næntʃl]	finanziell

Vocabulary 3

Everyday English: At a hotel

Die folgenden *phrases* helfen dir, wenn du auf Englisch ein Hotelzimmer buchst.

I would like to make a reservation, please.	Ich möchte ein Zimmer reservieren.
Do you have any rooms available?	Haben Sie freie Zimmer?
I would like a single room with a bath.	Ich hätte gerne ein Einzelzimmer mit Bad.
I would like a double room with a shower.	Ich hätte gerne ein Doppelzimmer mit Dusche.
I would like a twin room.	Ich hätte gerne ein Zweibettzimmer.
I'd like to stay for three nights from 10th June.	Ich möchte gerne für drei Nächte bleiben und zwar ab dem 10. Juni.
I'll be arriving at about six pm.	Ich komme gegen 18 Uhr an.
How much will the room cost?	Wie viel kostet das Zimmer?
Is breakfast included in the price?	Ist das Frühstück mit im Preis enthalten?
I'd like a non-smoking room, please.	Ich hätte gerne ein Nichtraucherzimmer.
What time is breakfast served?	Um wie viel Uhr gibt es Frühstück?
All our rooms have an en suite bathroom.	Unsere Zimmer sind alle mit Bad.
The room will cost £60 per person per night.	Das Zimmer kostet 60 Pfund pro Person pro Nacht.

network	['netwɜːk]	Netzwerk
unfortunately	[ʌn'fɔːtʃnətli]	leider; unglücklicherweise
compartment	[kəm'pɑːtmənt]	Zugabteil
shopping mall	['ʃɒpɪŋ ˌmɔːl]	Einkaufszentrum
slum	[slʌm]	Slum, Elendsviertel
hardly	['hɑːdli]	kaum
to **afford**	[ə'fɔːd]	sich leisten

economy [ɪˈkɒnəmi]	Wirtschaft
backpacker [ˈbækpækə]	Rucksacktourist/-in
highlight [ˈhaɪlaɪt]	Highlight, Höhepunkt
arrival [əˈraɪvl]	Ankunft(-s)
non-smoking [ˌnɒnˈsməʊkɪŋ]	Nichtraucher-
single room [ˌsɪŋgl ˈruːm]	Einzelzimmer
twin room [ˌtwɪn ˈruːm]	Zweibettzimmer
triple room [ˌtrɪpl ˈruːm]	Dreibettzimmer
en suite bathroom [ˌɒn swiːt ˈbɑːθrʊm]	Zimmer mit Bad
air conditioning [ˈeə kənˌdɪʃnɪŋ]	Klimaanlage
cable [ˈkeɪbl]	Kabel
to make a reservation [meɪk ə ˌrezəˈveɪʃn]	reservieren, eine Reservierung vornehmen
location [ləʊˈkeɪʃn]	Standort, Lage; Location; Drehort *(Film)*

Language 2

prayer [preə]	Gebet
guide [gaɪd]	Führer/-in
emperor [ˈemprə]	Kaiser
to bury [ˈberi]	begraben, beerdigen
marble (no pl.) [ˈmɑːbl]	Marmor
dawn [dɔːn]	Morgendämmerung, Tagesanbruch
fairy tale [ˈfeəri ˌteɪl]	Märchen
to study [ˈstʌdi]	studieren; lernen

Aspects

review [rɪˈvjuː]	Kritik, Rezension
complicated [ˈkɒmplɪkeɪtɪd]	kompliziert
subtitle [ˈsʌbˌtaɪtl]	Untertitel
fashion [ˈfæʃn]	Mode
sari [ˈsɑːri]	*indisches Kleidungsstück für Frauen*
kurta [ˈkɜːtə]	*weites, kragenloses Hemd für Männer*

Vocabulary 3

salwar kameez [ˌsælwɑː kəˈmiːz]	*aus zwei Teilen bestehendes Kleidungsstück für Männer und Frauen*
latest [ˈleɪtɪst]	neueste/-r/-s
selection [sɪˈlekʃn]	Auswahl
bracelet [ˈbreɪslət]	Armband
necklace [ˈnekləs]	Halskette
taste [teɪst]	Geschmack
superpower [ˈsuːpəˌpaʊə]	Supermacht
spice [spaɪs]	Gewürz
Portuguese [ˌpɔːtʃəˈgiːz]	portugiesisch, Portugiesisch; Portugiese/Portugiesin
settler [ˈsetlə]	Siedler/-in
cotton [ˈkɒtn]	Baumwolle
soldier [ˈsəʊldʒə]	Soldat/-in
ally [ˈælaɪ]	Verbündete(r)
soul [səʊl]	Seele
to **lead, led, led** [liːd, led, led]	führen
peaceful [ˈpiːsfl]	friedlich
campaign [kæmˈpeɪn]	Kampagne; Aktion
independence (no pl.) [ˌɪndɪˈpendənts]	Unabhängigkeit
to **matter** [ˈmætə]	von Bedeutung sein
jungle [ˈdʒʌŋgl]	Dschungel
to **sprint** [sprɪnt]	sprinten; spurten
fur [fɜː]	*hier:* Fell; Pelz
medicine [ˈmedsn]	Medizin
reserve [rɪˈzɜːv]	Reservat
environmentalist [ɪnˌvaɪərnˈmentlɪst]	Umweltschützer/-in
to **survive** [səˈvaɪv]	überleben
to **outsource** [ˈaʊtsɔːs]	outsourcen *(Ausgliedern von Produktions- oder Dienstleistungen an Externe)*
cost [kɒst]	Preis; Kosten
low [ləʊ]	niedrig
struggle [ˈstrʌgl]	Kampf; Anstrengung
belief [bɪˈliːf]	Glaube, Überzeugung

Option 1

mixture ['mɪkstʃə]	Mischung, Gemisch, Mixtur
to release [rɪ'li:s]	veröffentlichen, herausbringen
to generate ['dʒenreɪt]	generieren, erzeugen
recent ['ri:snt]	kürzlich; neueste/-r/-s; letzte/-r/-s
unusual [ʌn'ju:ʒl]	ungewöhnlich
to appear [ə'pɪə]	*hier:* auftreten; erscheinen
value ['vælju:]	Wert
common ['kɒmən]	gebräuchlich, verbreitet
corrupt [kə'rʌpt]	korrupt
politician [ˌpɒlɪ'tɪʃn]	Politiker/-in
to separate ['sepreɪt]	trennen
kidnap(ping) ['kɪdnæp(ɪŋ)]	Entführung, Kidnapping
emotional [ɪ'məʊʃnl]	emotional; gefühlsmäßig
masala [mə'sɑ:lə]	*indische Gewürzmischung*
the press [pres]	die Presse
to star [stɑ:]	die Hauptrolle spielen *(Film, Theater)*
to nominate ['nɒmɪneɪt]	nominieren, vorschlagen
influence ['ɪnfluənts]	Einfluss
storyline ['stɔ:rilaɪn]	Handlung
to research [rɪ'sɜ:tʃ]	recherchieren; erforschen; untersuchen

Option 2

out of [ˌaʊt'əv]	aus
accessory [ək'sesri]	Accessoire *(modisches Zubehör)*
outfit (no pl.) ['aʊtfɪt]	Outfit, Kleidung
fashionable ['fæʃnəbl]	modisch; elegant
silk [sɪlk]	Seide
pattern ['pætn]	Muster
waist [weɪst]	Bauch; Taille
loose [lu:s]	locker; lose
bangle ['bæŋgl]	Armreif

mangalasutra [ˌmæŋɡələˈsuːtrə]	*besondere indische Halskette*
wedding [ˈwedɪŋ]	Hochzeit
ring [rɪŋ]	Ring
husband [ˈhʌzbənd]	Ehemann
pyjamas pl. [pɪˈʤɑːməz]	Schlafanzug, Pyjama
tight [taɪt]	fest, eng
ankle [ˈæŋkl]	Fußknöchel
waistline [ˈweɪstlaɪn]	Taille
tikka [ˈtɪkə]	*hier: trad. ind. Haar-Accessoire*
the **high street** [ˈhaɪ ˌstriːt]	die Haupteinkaufsstraße
exception [ɪkˈsepʃn]	Ausnahme
hoodie [ˈhʊdi]	Kapuzenjacke/-shirt
profit [ˈprɒfɪt]	Profit; Gewinn
wide [waɪd]	groß; breit; weit
plain [pleɪn]	klar; schlicht; einfach
catalogue [ˈkætlɒɡ]	Katalog

Pair words

Paarwörter, wie *trousers*, *jeans*, *glasses*, bezeichnen Dinge, die aus zwei Teilen bestehen (z. B. zwei Hosenbeinen). Sie werden immer nur im Plural verwendet:

*Your new **jeans** look really nice. Where did you buy **them**?*
*Have you seen my **sunglasses**? I can't find **them**.*

Möchtest du über <u>eine</u> Brille, Hose usw. sprechen, verwendest du *a pair of* oder *some*:

*I bought **a** new **pair of** sunglasses yesterday.*
*He wore **some** old jeans to the party.*

Option 3

tourism ['tʊərɪzm]	Tourismus
central ['sentrl]	zentral
jeep [dʒiːp]	Jeep, Geländewagen
core [kɔː]	Kern
vehicle ['vɪəkl]	Fahrzeug; Vehikel
to **reach** [riːtʃ]	erreichen
to **locate** [ləʊ'keɪt]	orten, lokalisieren
packaged ['pækɪdʒd]	abgepackt; *hier:* unecht, künstlich
mahout [mə'haʊt]	*Elefantenhüter/-in in Indien*
pool [puːl]	Schwimmbecken, *hier:* Tümpel
lazy ['leɪzi]	faul
ritual ['rɪtjuəl]	Ritual
thrill [θrɪl]	Nervenkitzel
to **sight** [saɪt]	sichten
nevertheless [ˌnevəðə'les]	nichtsdestoweniger, trotzdem
public holiday [ˌpʌblɪk 'hɒlədeɪ]	gesetzl. Feiertag
tigress ['taɪgres]	Tigerin
cub [kʌb]	Junge(s)
to **be about to do s.th.** [bi ə'baʊt tə]	im Begriff sein, etw. zu tun
deer pl. deer [dɪə]	Hirsch, Reh; Rotwild
jaws pl. [dʒɔːz]	Maul
fawn [fɔːn]	Rehkitz, Hirschkalb
moment of a lifetime ['laɪftaɪm]	einmalige Chance
alarm (no pl.) [ə'lɑːm]	Alarm, Besorgnis
rate [reɪt]	Rate
hunt [hʌnt]	Jagd
frustration [frʌs'treɪʃn]	Frust, Enttäuschung, Frustration
unlike [ʌn'laɪk]	anders als, im Gegensatz zu
expert ['ekspɜːt]	Experte/Expertin

practice ['præktɪs]	*hier:* Sitte; Praktik; Gewohnheit
optimistic [ˌɒptɪ'mɪstɪk]	optimistisch
corridor ['kɒrɪdɔ:]	Gang, Flur, Korridor
approach [ə'prəʊtʃ]	Ansatz
wildcat ['waɪldkæt]	Wildkatze
endangered [ɪn'deɪndʒəd]	gefährdet
species pl. **species** ['spi:ʃi:z]	Art, Spezies

Wordwise

anagram ['ænəgræm]	Anagramm *(Buchstabendreher)*

Exercises with words from Check-in to Aspects

1 Opposites

Wie lautet das Gegenteil dieser Wörter? Tipp: Alle gesuchten Wörter stammen aus Topic 3.

1. high ↔ _____

2. easy ↔ _____

3. empty ↔ _____

4. oldest ↔ _____

5. enemy ↔ _____

6. to die ↔ _____

3 Exercises

2 New words

Ergänze die folgenden Wortanfänge so, dass Wörter aus Topic 3 entstehen. Schreibe auch die deutsche Übersetzung dazu.

1. net_____

2. form_____

3. soft_____

4. text_____

5. super_____

6. in_____

7. cloth_____

8. rick_____

9. sub_____

10. high_____

11. neck_____

12. engine_____

13. environment_____

14. to out_____

15. back_____

16. late_____

Exercises 3

3 Word families

Welches Wort aus Topic 3 passt in die jeweilige Wortfamilie?

1. clothes _____

2. to arrive _____

3. crowd _____

4. religion _____

5. to taste _____

6. peace _____

7. independent _____

8. environment _____

9. to believe _____

4 Definitions

Erkläre diese drei Begriffe auf Englisch.

1. rupee _____

_____

2. dish _____

_____

3. tie _____

_____

45

5 Matching verbs

Ordne die Verben den deutschen Übersetzungen zu.

1. to afford
2. to make a reservation
3. to bury
4. to study
5. to lead
6. to matter
7. to survive
8. to sprint

a) begraben, beerdigen
b) führen
c) spurten
d) reservieren
e) überleben
f) sich leisten
g) von Bedeutung sein
h) studieren; lernen

6 Word lines

Welche Wörter aus Topic 3 passen ...

a) ... inhaltlich in die jeweilige Reihe?

1. earring, necklace, _____

2. dress, jeans, _____

3. dollar, euro, _____

4. cow, pig, _____

b) ... der Endung nach in die jeweilige Reihe?
Finde zwei Wörter pro Endung.

1. -ian: _____

2. -ion: _____

3. -al: _____

4. -ly: _____

Exercises 3

7 Which word?

Ergänze die Sätze mit dem richtigen Wort.

1. I love the colour of spices but I don't like the _____.
   taste   soul   review   cotton

2. Shirts and T-shirts are often made of _____.
   jungle   cotton   spices   marble

3. People in church say _____ together.
   settlers   kurtas   saris   prayers

4. Areas with lots of cities are _____ populated.
   hardly   latest   peacefully   densely

5. It doesn't _____ how rich you are.
   sprint   cost   matter   income

6. A _____ is a safe place for animals.
   belief   reserve   dawn   necklace

7. You wear a _____ on your arm.
   sari   salwar kameez   necklace   bracelet

8. A _____ usually has a happy ending.
   location   fairy tale   slum   network

8 The letter 'o'

In all diesen Wörtern kommt der Buchstabe ‚o' vor, aber er wird nicht immer gleich ausgesprochen. Sortiere die Wörter.

port   ox   software   formerly   location   cost
hot   Portuguese   compartment   economy   low
major   religious   clothing   soldier   to afford

[ɒ]

_____

_____

_____

_____

[ə]

_____

_____

_____

_____

[ɔː]

_____

_____

_____

_____

[əʊ]

_____

_____

_____

_____

Exercises for Option 1

9 Lost vowels

In diesen Wörtern aus Option 1 fehlen die Vokale.
Setze sie wieder richtig ein und finde so das versteckte Wort.
Es bezeichnet einen Beruf.

						1.	P	R		S	S	
					2.	C		M	M		N	
				3.	V		L					
4.	S	T		R	Y	L		N				
				5.	S	T		R				
				6.	K		D	N		P		
7.	R		S			R	C	H				
	8.		M		T			N		L		
		9.	M		S		L					
	10.	R		C		N	T					

10 What am I?

1. My first is in politician but not in corrupt. ____

2. My second is in kidnap and in press. ____

3. My third is in separate but not in research. ____

4. My fourth is in value but not in star. ____

5. My fifth is in star and in value. ____

6. My sixth is in storyline but not in influence. ____

When someone or something is suddenly there, they

_____

3 Exercises

Exercise for Option 2

11 What is it?

Welche Wörter werden hier gesucht?

1. You wear a _____ on your finger.

2. _____ is the opposite of wife.

3. When two people marry, the event is called a _____.

4. Men and women can wear _____ when they go to bed.

5. You can order things (clothes, furniture, books) from a _____ and you don't need to go to the shops.

6. These trousers are too _____ around my waist, I can't breathe.

7. A _____ is the money that a company has earned when all the bills have been paid.

8. This table is too _____, it won't fit in here.

9. Look at my _____! I shouldn't have eaten all that chocolate at Christmas – I must go on a diet.

10. Your _____ is the part of your body that joins your leg with your foot.

Exercises for Option 3

12 Almost the same!

Notiere die englischen Übersetzungen. Achte dabei auf die kleinen Unterschiede in der Schreibung.

1. Tourismus = _____

2. zentral = _____

3. Experte / Expertin = _____

4. optimistisch = _____

5. Wildkatze = _____

6. Spezies = _____

7. lokalisieren = _____

8. Vehikel = _____

13 First letters

Schreibe alle Wörter aus Option 3 auf, die mit diesen Buchstaben anfangen.

R _____

E _____

A _____

C _____

H _____

Exercise for all of Topic 3

14 Word puzzle

Übersetze die deutschen Wörter ins Englische und suche dann die englischen Wörter im Gitternetz.

1. Ausnahme _____
2. Anstrengung _____
3. durchschnittlich _____
4. Wirtschaft _____
5. Ankunft _____
6. Kaiser _____
7. Marmor _____
8. Morgendämmerung _____
9. Kritik _____
10. Mode _____
11. Auswahl _____
12. Kleidung _____
13. scharf _____
14. Hafen(stadt) _____
15. Fell; Pelz _____

N	S	T	R	U	G	G	L	E	F	U	R
E	M	P	E	R	O	R	F	D	A	W	N
V	O	U	T	F	I	T	R	A	S	E	M
E	M	A	R	B	L	E	U	R	H	C	U
R	E	V	I	E	W	S	S	R	I	O	E
T	L	E	X	C	E	P	T	I	O	N	M
H	W	R	C	U	H	P	R	V	N	O	O
E	A	A	A	R	O	O	A	A	J	M	T
L	I	G	B	R	T	R	T	L	U	Y	I
E	S	E	L	E	C	T	I	O	N	A	O

Topic 4 Choices and decisions

Check-in

decision [dɪˈsɪʒn]	Entscheidung
in the time ahead [əˈhed]	in der Zukunft
difficulty [ˈdɪfɪklti]	Schwierigkeit
quarrel [ˈkwɒrəl]	Streit, Auseinandersetzung
wheelchair [ˈwiːltʃeə]	Rollstuhl
homeless [ˈhəʊmləs]	obdachlos
message [ˈmesɪdʒ]	*hier:* Botschaft
to **manage to (do s.th.)** [ˈmænɪdʒ]	schaffen (etw. zu tun)
operation [ˌɒpˈreɪʃn]	Operation
mental [ˈmentl]	geistig
physical [ˈfɪzɪkl]	physisch, körperlich

---

the + adjective

Wenn du über eine gesamte Gruppe von Menschen sprechen möchtest, benutzt du *the + adjective,* z. B. *the poor* (= alle Armen).

*There should be more opportunities for **the young**.*
*Oxfam is a charity which tries to help **the poor**.*
*Have you ever seen the film **The Good, the Bad and the Ugly**?*
*We should care more for **the homeless**.*

Language

straight [streɪt]	*hier:* sofort
lunchbox [ˈlʌntʃbɒks]	Brotdose, Lunchbox
mould [məʊld]	Schimmel
Yuck! [jʌk]	Igitt!
to **impress** [ɪmˈpres]	beeindrucken
hardly [ˈhɑːdli]	kaum
to **mean (to do s.th.)** [miːn]	beabsichtigen (etw. zu tun)

4 Vocabulary

Aspects

table ['teɪbl]	*hier:* Tabelle
employment (no pl.) [ɪm'plɔɪmənt]	Beschäftigung; Anstellung
age of consent [ˌeɪdʒ əv kən'sent]	(Ehe-)Mündigkeitsalter
consent [kən'sent]	Zustimmung, Einwilligung
sex [seks]	*hier:* Sex, Sexualität; Geschlecht
marriage ['mærɪdʒ]	Heirat; Ehe
male [meɪl]	männlich
illegal [ɪ'liːgl]	illegal; rechtswidrig
criminal ['krɪmɪnl]	kriminell, verbrecherisch
spirits pl. ['spɪrɪts]	Spirituosen
compulsory [kəm'pʌlsri]	verpflichtend; obligatorisch
rise (no pl.) [raɪz]	*hier:* Anstieg; Aufstieg
anorexia (nervosa) [ˌænrˌeksiə nɜː'vəʊzə]	Magersucht
to publish ['pʌblɪʃ]	veröffentlichen; publizieren; verlegen
record ['rekɔːd]	*hier:* Rekord(-)
eating disorder ['iːtɪŋ dɪˌsɔːdə]	Essstörung
to admit s.o. to hospital [əd'mɪt]	jdn. ins Krankenhaus einliefern
common ['kɒmən]	gebräuchlich, *hier:* verbreitet
slimmer ['slɪmə]	figurbewusste Person
disease [dɪ'ziːz]	Krankheit
fat [fæt]	fett, dick
to starve [stɑːv]	(ver)hungern
to be/become aware of s.th. [ə'weə]	sich einer Sache bewusst sein/werden
illness ['ɪlnəs]	Krankheit
sixth form ['sɪksθ ˌfɔːm]	Oberstufe
further education college [fɜːðə edjuː'keɪʃn ˌkɒlɪdʒ]	*eine Art Berufsschule*
specialist ['speʃlɪst]	Spezial-, Fach-
such as ['sʌtʃ əz]	wie (zum Beispiel)
horticulture ['hɔːtɪkʌltʃə]	Gartenbau

agriculture ['ægrɪkʌltʃə]	Landwirtschaft
... as well as ... [əz 'wel əz]	sowohl ... als auch ...
study ['stʌdi]	Lernen, Studieren
specific [spə'sɪfɪk]	spezifisch, speziell
to prepare [prɪ'peə]	*hier:* vorbereiten; sich vorbereiten auf; zubereiten
self-employment [ˌselfɪm'plɔɪmənt]	Selbstständigkeit
kindergarten ['kɪndəgɑːtn]	Kindergarten
vet [vet]	Tierarzt/Tierärztin

Option 1

apart [ə'pɑːt]	auseinander, getrennt
shiny ['ʃaɪni]	glänzend
chorus ['kɔːrəs]	Refrain
to shine, shone, shone [ʃaɪn, ʃɒn, ʃɒn]	*hier:* scheinen; glänzen
to take an oath [əʊθ]	einen Eid schwören
to stick, stuck, stuck s.th. out [stɪk, stʌk, stʌk]	einer Sache treu bleiben
till [tɪl]	bis
fancy ['fæntsi]	ausgefallen
entity ['entɪti]	Einheit; *hier:* Existenz
infinity (no pl.) [ɪn'fɪnəti]	Unendlichkeit
to deal, dealt, dealt [diːl, delt, delt]	austeilen
alarmed [ə'lɑːmd]	beunruhigt, besorgt
distance ['dɪstnts]	Distanz, Entfernung
to pour [pɔː]	einschenken, eingießen; *hier:* schütten
Caribbean [ˌkærɪ'biːən]	karibisch
Grammy ['græmi]	Grammy *(musikal. Auszeichnung)*
ordinary ['ɔːdnri]	einfach, herkömmlich, normal
fanclub ['fænˌklʌb]	Fanklub
paintstained [ˌpeɪnt'steɪnd]	mit Farbe beschmiert
blanket ['blæŋkɪt]	(Woll-)Decke

delight [dɪ'laɪt]	Vergnügen, Entzücken
to **put out** [ˌpʊt ˈaʊt]	ausschalten, löschen
Top of the Pops [ˌtɒp əv ðə 'pɒps]	*Name einer Hitparade im Fernsehen; hier:* gut drauf
panty ['pænti]	Slip
forlorn [fəˈlɔːn]	einsam, verlassen
nightdress ['naɪtdres]	Nachthemd
slightly ['slaɪtli]	ein wenig, etwas
dawn [dɔːn]	Morgendämmerung, Tagesanbruch
friendship ['frendʃɪp]	Freundschaft

Option 2

to **be dying to do s.th.** ['daɪɪŋ]	unbedingt etw. machen wollen
anorexic [ˌænrˈeksɪk]	magersüchtig
to **beat** [biːt]	*hier:* besiegen
bank [bæŋk]	Bank
yet [jet]	*hier:* und trotzdem, und dennoch
tube [tjuːb]	Schlauch
worthless ['wɜːθləs]	wertlos
to **keep** (+ *adj.*) [kiːp]	*hier:* bleiben
to **creep, crept, crept up** [kriːp, krept, krept]	hinaufkriechen, hinaufsteigen
jacket potato [ˌdʒækɪt pəˈteɪtəʊ]	Folien-, Ofenkartoffel
to **consist of** [kənˈsɪst əv]	bestehen aus
sip [sɪp]	kleiner Schluck
constant ['kɒnstənt]	ständig, konstant, stetig, gleichmäßig
to **lie** [laɪ]	lügen
certain ['sɜːtn]	*hier:* bestimmt; sicher
withdrawn [wɪðˈdrɔːn]	introvertiert
to **cuddle** ['kʌdl]	kuscheln, knuddeln
moody ['muːdi]	launisch, ausausgeglichen
to **diagnose s.th.** ['daɪgnəʊz]	etw. diagnostizieren, feststellen

to **deny** [dɪ'naɪ]	abstreiten
sensible ['sensɪbl]	vernünftig
condition [kən'dɪʃn]	*hier:* Zustand, Verfassung
a while [ə 'waɪl]	eine Weile
model ['mɒdl]	Model
patient ['peɪʃnt]	Patient/-in
out-patient ['aʊtˌpeɪʃnt]	ambulanter Patient/ ambulante Patientin
unit ['juːnɪt]	*hier:* Abteilung *(auf einer Krankenstation)*
before long [bɪ'fɔː]	schon bald
liquid ['lɪkwɪd]	flüssig
expert ['ekspɜːt]	fachmännisch, erfahren
care [keə]	Pflege, Behandlung, Betreuung
treatment ['triːtmənt]	Behandlung
therapy ['θerəpi]	Therapie
to **discharge s.o.** [dɪs'tʃɑːdʒ]	jdn. aus dem Krankenhaus entlassen
ambassador [æm'bæsədə]	Botschafter/-in
mealtime ['miːltaɪm]	Essenszeit
milestone ['maɪlstəʊn]	Meilenstein
to **recover** [rɪ'kʌvə]	sich erholen
to **turn to s.th./s.o.** ['tɜːn tə]	sich etw./jdm. zuwenden
to **lead, led, led** [liːd, led, led]	führen
publication [ˌpʌblɪ'keɪʃn]	Veröffentlichung, Publikation
link [lɪŋk]	Link, Verbindung

Option 3

automotive [ˌɔːtə'məʊtɪv]	Auto-, Fahrzeug-
internship *(AE)* ['ɪntɜːnʃɪp]	Praktikum
department [dɪ'pɑːtmənt]	Abteilung
manufacturing (no pl.) [ˌmænjə'fæktʃrɪŋ]	Herstellung, Fertigung
Human Resources [ˌhjuːmən rɪ'zɔːsɪz]	Personalwesen

Talking about strengths and weaknesses

Die folgenden *phrases* können dir helfen, wenn du über deine Stärken *(strengths)* und Schwächen *(weaknesses)* sprechen möchtest.

I think / I'd say I'm reliable [rɪ'laɪəbl] */ creative / practical* ['præktɪkl] */ … .*	Ich denke / Ich würde sagen, dass ich zuverlässig / kreativ / praktisch veranlagt / … bin.
I find (don't find) it easy to meet people / to learn new skills / …	Es fällt mir leicht (nicht leicht), neue Menschen kennenzulernen / Ich habe eine schnelle Auffassungsgabe / …
I'm (not so) good with animals / children / my hands / …	Ich bin (nicht so) gut im Umgang mit Tieren / mit Kindern / Ich bin (nicht) sehr praktisch veranlagt / …
I prefer to work alone / outside / with my hands / … .	Ich ziehe es vor, alleine / draußen / mit meinen Händen / … zu arbeiten.
I don't like computers / offices / working outside in bad weather / …	Ich mag keine Computer / keine Büros / Bei schlechtem Wetter möchte ich nicht draußen arbeiten / …

development [dɪ'veləpmənt]	Entwicklung
marketing (no pl.) ['mɑːkɪtɪŋ]	Marketing, Vermarktung
sales [seɪlz]	Vertrieb, Verkauf
finance ['faɪnænts]	Finanzwesen, Finanzen; Finanz-
public relations (PR) [ˌpʌblɪk rɪ'leɪʃnz]	Öffentlichkeitsarbeit
chief executive officer (CEO) [ˌtʃiːf ɪgˌzekjətɪv 'ɒfɪsə]	Generaldirektor/-in; Geschäftsführer/-in

junior ['ʤuːniə]	Junior, der Jüngere
to develop [dɪ'veləp]	(sich) entwickeln
electric [ɪ'lektrɪk]	elektrisch
vehicle ['vɪəkl]	Fahrzeug; Vehikel
fashion ['fæʃn]	Mode
great-grandson [ˌgreɪt'grænsʌn]	Urenkel
production (no pl.) [prə'dʌkʃn]	Herstellung, Produktion
manufacturer [ˌmænjə'fæktʃərə]	Hersteller/-in
employee [ɪm'plɔɪiː]	Angestellter/Angestellte; Mitarbeiter/-in
based (in) [beɪst]	ansässig (in)

Adjectives with prefixes

Du kannst einige Vorsilben *(prefixes)* an Adjektive anhängen, um ein Adjektiv mit der gegenteiligen Bedeutung zu bilden.

Mit der Vorsilbe *un-* klappt es in den meisten Fällen:

→ ***un**usual*	ungewöhnlich
→ ***un**funny*	nicht lustig
→ ***un**important*	unwichtig
→ ***un**comfortable*	unbequem
→ ***un**helpful*	nicht hilfreich; nicht hilfsbereit

Bei manchen Adjektiven brauchst du jedoch *in-*, *im-* oder sogar *il-*. Versuche dir diese Fälle zu merken:

→ ***in**correct*	falsch, fehlerhaft
→ ***in**direct*	indirekt
→ ***im**possible*	unmöglich
→ ***im**practical* [ɪm'præktɪkl]	unpraktisch
→ ***il**legal*	illegal
→ ***il**logical* [ɪ'lɒʤɪkl]	unlogisch

sector ['sektə]	Sektor, Abschnitt, (Unternehmens-) Bereich
financial [faɪ'nænt∫l]	finanziell
to manufacture [ˌmænjə'fækt∫ə]	fertigen, herstellen, produzieren
to service ['sɜːvɪs]	überprüfen, warten
to market ['mɑːkɪt]	vermarkten, vertreiben
dealer ['diːlə]	Händler/-in
to supply [sə'plaɪ]	(be)liefern, ausrüsten
rental ['rentl]	Miet-, Verleih-
leasing ['liːsɪŋ]	Leasing
after-sales service [ɑːftə'seɪlz ˌsɜːvɪs]	Kundendienst
repair [rɪ'peə]	Reparatur
loan [ləʊn]	Darlehen, Kredit
insurance [ɪn'∫ʊərns]	Versicherung
unpaid [ʌn'peɪd]	unbezahlt
to employ [ɪm'plɔɪ]	einstellen, beschäftigen
damage assessment [ˌdæmɪdʒ ə'sesmənt]	Schadensfeststellung, Schadensbemessung
damage ['dæmɪdʒ]	Schaden, Beschädigung
assessment [ə'sesmənt]	Bewertung, Einschätzung
prototype ['prəʊtətaɪp]	Prototyp
dimension [ˌdaɪ'men∫n]	Dimension
flexible ['fleksɪbl]	flexibel, beweglich
excellent ['ekslnt]	exzellent, hervorragend
to photocopy ['fəʊtəʊˌkɒpi]	(foto)kopieren
organizational [ˌɔːgnaɪ'zeɪ∫nl]	organisatorisch
brand [brænd]	Marke(n-)
fictional ['fɪk∫nl]	erfunden, fiktiv

Wordwise

boss [bɒs]	Boss, Chef

Check-out

souvenir [ˌsuːvə'nɪə]	Souvenir, Andenken
unfortunately [ʌn'fɔːt∫nətli]	leider; unglücklicherweise

Exercises with words from Check-in to Aspects

1 Definitions

Erkläre diese sechs Begriffe auf Englisch.

1. disease: _____

   _____

   _____

2. operation: _____

   _____

   _____

3. mould: _____

   _____

   _____

4. hardly: _____

   _____

   _____

5. spirits: _____

   _____

   _____

6. rise: _____

   _____

   _____

2 New expressions

Kombiniere jeweils zwei Wörter aus Topic 4, um einen neuen Ausdruck zu erhalten. Achte beim Schreiben darauf, ob die Wörter getrennt, zusammen oder mit Bindestrich geschrieben werden.

lunch   employment   chair   form   self   nervosa

anorexia   disorder   box   wheel   eating   sixth

1. _____

2. _____

3. _____

4. _____

5. _____

6. _____

3 One word – two meanings

Diese englischen Wörter aus Topic 4 haben im Deutschen zwei Bedeutungen, die z. T. ganz unterschiedlich sind. Schreibe zu jedem Begriff zwei deutsche Übersetzungen auf.

1. table: _____

2. message: _____

3. straight: _____

4 Wordbuilding

Ergänze die folgende Tabelle.

Verb	Noun	Adjective
to decide	1.	–
–	2.	difficult
3.	manager	–
to marry	4.	5.
--	crime	6.
to rise	7.	–
8.	impression	–
–	9.	ill

5 Matching verbs

Ordne den Verben die deutschen Übersetzungen zu.

1. to mean (to do s.th.)
2. to publish
3. to starve
4. to prepare
5. to be aware of s.th.
6. to admit s.o. to hospital
7. to impress
8. to manage to (do s.th.)

a) (ver)hungern
b) vorbereiten; zubereiten
c) jdn. ins Krankenhaus einliefern
d) beabsichtigen (etw. zu tun)
e) schaffen (etw. zu tun)
f) sich einer Sache bewusst sein
g) veröffentlichen; verlegen
h) beeindrucken

4 Exercises

6 Word lines

Welches Wort aus Topic 4 passt ...

a) *... inhaltlich in die jeweilige Reihe?*

1. pencil case, exercise book, _____

2. boy, man, _____

3. doctor, nurse, _____

4. for example, e.g., _____

b) *... der Endung nach in die jeweilige Reihe?
Finde zwei Wörter pro Endung.*

1. -ion: _____

2. -al: _____

3. -ure: _____

4. -ess: _____

7 Sounds

Übertrage diese Wörter aus der Lautschrift.

1. [ˈrekɔːd]: _____
2. [spəˈsɪfɪk]: _____
3. [ˈspeʃlɪst]: _____
4. [ˈkɪndəgɑːtn]: _____
5. [ˈstʌdi]: _____
6. [ˌɒprˈeɪʃn]: _____
7. [ˈkɒmən]: _____
8. [ˈslɪmə]: _____
9. [meɪl]: _____
10. [kənˈsent]: _____

Exercises 4

8 Which word?

Ergänze die Sätze mit dem richtigen Wort.

1. He wants to be a farmer, so he has to learn all about _____.

   agriculture   self-employment   illness   horticulture

2. You are not allowed to buy _____ until you are 18.

   records   studies   tables   spirits

3. At 16 you have to make a lot of important _____ .

   employment   studies   elections   decisions

4. In Germany 18 is the legal age for _____ .

   sixth forms   marriage   decisions   quarrels

5. When you ride a motorcycle it is _____ to wear a helmet.

   illegal   criminal   compulsory   physical

6. The bread was over a week old and there was green _____ all over it.

   grass   leaves   mould   fat

7. You go to the _____ if your dog or cat is ill.

   vet   doctor   farmer   nurse

8. I don't wear pyjamas, I wear a _____ .

   blanket   nightdress   friendship   illness

4 Exercises

Exercise for Option 1

9 Word puzzle

Finde die folgenden Wörter aus Topic 4, die im Gitternetz versteckt sind. Die Buchstaben, die übrig bleiben, ergeben den kompletten Namen der Sängerin des Songs „Umbrella":

_____

alarmed	blanket	chorus	dawn
deal	delight	distance	entity
fanclub	fancy	friendship	inifinity
nightdress	panty	paintstained	pour
shine	shiny	slightly	stick
stuck	till		

R	F	T	O	S	L	I	G	H	T	L	Y
P	A	I	N	T	S	T	A	I	N	E	D
A	N	L	B	I	H	Y	D	N	I	D	E
N	C	L	N	C	I	R	A	F	G	I	L
T	L	I	H	K	N	A	W	I	H	S	I
Y	U	N	F	N	E	A	N	N	T	T	G
S	B	L	A	N	K	E	T	I	D	A	H
T	F	E	N	T	I	T	Y	T	R	N	T
U	P	E	C	S	H	I	N	Y	E	C	D
C	O	N	Y	C	H	O	R	U	S	E	E
K	U	A	L	A	R	M	E	D	S	T	A
F	R	I	E	N	D	S	H	I	P	Y	L

66

Exercise for Option 2

10 Verbs, verbs, verbs

Wie heißen diese Verben aus Option 2 auf Englisch?

1. unbedingt etw. machen wollen =

   to _____

2. besiegen = to _____

3. bleiben = to _____

4. hinaufkriechen, hinaufsteigen = to _____

5. bestehen aus = to _____

6. lügen = to _____

7. kuscheln, knuddeln = to _____

8. etw. diagnostizieren, feststellen = to _____

9. abstreiten = to _____

10. jdn. aus dem Krankenhaus entlassen =

    to _____

11. sich erholen = to _____

12. sich etw. / jdm. zuwenden = to _____

13. führen = to _____

4 Exercises

Exercises for Option 3

11 First letters

Schreibe alle Wörter aus Option 3 auf, die mit den folgenden Buchstaben anfangen.

S _____

A _____

L _____

E _____

S _____

F _____

O _____

R _____

C _____

E _____

12 Almost the same!

Notiere die englischen Übersetzungen und achte dabei auf die kleinen Unterschiede in der Schreibung.

1. finanziell = _____

2. elektrisch = _____

3. organisatorisch = _____

4. Reparatur = _____

Exercise for all of Topic 4

13 What do you say?

Wie heißen diese Sätze auf Englisch? Übersetze sie.

1. Ich denke, dass ich kreativ bin.

   _____

2. Ich mag keine Computer und Büros.

   _____

3. Bei schlechtem Wetter möchte ich nicht draußen

   arbeiten. _____

   _____

4. Ich ziehe es vor, mit meinen Händen zu arbeiten.

   _____

   _____

5. Ich bin gut im Umgang mit Tieren.

   _____

6. Ich bin nicht sehr praktisch veranlagt.

   _____

7. Es fällt mir nicht leicht, neue Menschen

   kennenzulernen. _____

   _____

Puzzles

1 Cryptogram

Die Ziffern 1 – 20 in den Tabellen stehen für je einen Buchstaben. Finde zu jedem Topic heraus, welcher Satz oder Ausdruck sich hinter den Ziffern verbirgt. Viel Glück.

Beginning word:

17	1	14	11	3	11	4	2
D	E	C	I	S	I	O	N

1	2	3	4	5	6	7	8	9	10
E	N	S	O						
11	12	13	14	15	16	17	18	19	20
I			C			D			

Topic 1:

__ __ __ __ __ __ __ __ __
1 2 6 7 11 3 10   11 3

__ __ __ __ __ __
3 12 4 13 1 2

__ __ __ __ __ __ __ __ __ __ .
1 20 1 5 8 9 10 1 5 1

Topic 2:

__ __ __ __ __ __ __ __ __ __ __
14 10 15 2 6 1   9 1   14 15 2

__ __ __ __ __ __ __ __ __ .
16 1 7 11 1 20 1   11 2

| | Puzzles | P |

Topic 3:

__ __ __ __ __ __ __ __ __ __ __
10 4 7 7 8 9 4 4 17 4 5

__ __ __ __ __ __ __ __ _?_
16 4 7 7 8 9 4 4 17

Topic 4:

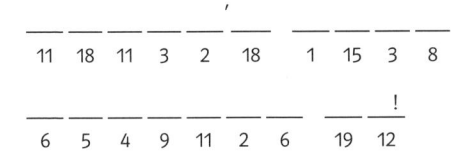

__ __ __ __ __ ,__ __ __ __ __
11 18 11 3 2 18 1 15 3 8

__ __ __ __ __ __ __ __ _!_
6 5 4 9 11 2 6 19 12

2 Irregular verbs

Wie lauten die fehlenden Verbformen zu diesen Verben?

infinitive	simple past	past participle
1. to spread	_____	_____
2. to lie	_____	_____
3. to lead	_____	_____
4. to shine	_____	_____

Topic 1

1　Languages

native speaker, Hindi, mother tongue, fluent, multi-lingual, Punjabi, Urdu, German, spoken, translation, words

2　Almost the same!

1. politician   2. call center   3. nationality
4. contact   5. chat room   6. interviewer   7. to note down   8. handball   9. professional   10. passion

3　Hyphen or no hyphen?

with hyphen: multi-lingual, non-official, home-made, full-time

without hyphen: mother tongue, call center, subcontinent, native speaker

4　Which word?

1. Inuktitut   2. backpacker   3. empire   4. smart
5. shower   6. fluent   7. departments

5　New words

1. coaching   2. talented   3. baggage   4. complaint
5. interviewer   6. delivery   7. nationality

6　Definitions

Vorschlag: 1. A person who speaks many languages fluently is multi-lingual.   2. They provide money for a certain group of people or for a special event.   3. Hinglish is a mixture of English with Hindi, Urdu and Punjabi.   4. When a lot of people have the same name, the name is common.

7　Opposites

a) 1. non-official   2. foreign language   3. interviewer
   4. immediately

b) *Vorschläge:* 1. to disrespect   2. to immigrate
   3. irregular   4. unlike / unhealthy / unhappy

8　What's the word?

1. permission   2. session   3. passion   4. to spread
5. multi-lingual   6. majority

9 Word lines
a) 1. Inuktitut 2. assassin 3. interviewer 4. shower
b) 1. admission 2. explorer 3. department 4. baggage

10 Matching verbs
1. f) 2. d) 3. h) 4. c) 5. g) 6. a) 7. b) 8. e)

11 What do you say?
1. I only used to speak my mother tongue, Inuktitut.
2. I work for a company that has spread quickly.
3. My 'dream' job would be as an explorer. 4. Can you describe yourself, please? 5. I like working with my hands. 6. My hobbies are cycling and swimming 7. I did my final exams last year.

12 Odd one out
a) whatever; webzine; Cape Town; former; university
b) football; adjectives; languages; people; schools

13 Endings
1. Cantonese, *Vorschlag:* Chinese 2. scholarship, *Vorschlag:* relationship 3. bilingual, multi-lingual, *Vorschlag:* casual 4. (to be) hopeless, *Vorschlag:* helpless

14 Sounds
1. secondary school; weiterführende Schule
2. storyboard; Storyboard 3. review; Kritik, Rezension 4. (to) emigrate; emigrieren, auswandern

15 Which word?
1. storyboard 2. mangas 3. elementary 4. talent

16 Word groups
1. screenager 2. among 3. exaggerated 4. hood
5. bit 6. exist 7. catch 8. homie 9. collage
10. search

17 Personal qualities
Deine eigenen Wörter und Sätze

Topic 2

1 **Matching verbs**
1. d) 2. a) 3. e) 4. b) 5. c)

2 **GB or USA?**
GB: House of Lords, House of Commons, queen / king, prime minister, monarch, candidate
USA: House of Representatives, president, senator, the Senate, Congress, candidate

3 **Matching words**
head of state / government, no longer, chat room, among others, voting station, Member of Parliament, motorway

4 **One word, two meanings**
1. valid 2. pub 3. to break up s.th. 4. previous
5. representative 6. message 7. to hide s.th.

5 **Definitions**
Vorschlag: 1. The countryside is land with trees, lakes and fields outside of towns. 2. A campaign is when you protest and give your opinion about something.
3. This is when s.o. brings s.th. for you. 4. A high turnout at an election means that a lot of people voted.

6 **The correct meaning**
1. a) 2. a) 3. b) 4. a) 5. b) 6. a)

7 **Word lines**
a) 1. motorway 2. pub 3. message
b) 1. peaceful 2. demonstration 3. politician
   4. illegal 5. replacement 6. senator

8 **Sounds**
1. politician 2. candidate 3. pub 4. troops
5. minister 6. tear gas 7. court 8. valid
9. disturb 10. hoodie

9 What do you say?

1. I think our government is good.   2. I think everyone in our society / each member of our society should vote.   3. I think that young people should feel responsible for the environment.   4. In my opinion the biggest problem is pollution.   5. I'm glad we don't have a war in our country.   6. If I was in the government, I would fight for more schools.

10 Word puzzle

→: confidential, corridor, monarchy, ambassador, join, occasionally

↓: crossword, husband, throne, likely, wake, tray

↘: political, patron, chambermaid, honour, matter, social

Lösungswort: The President of the US

11 Verbs, verbs, verbs

1. speculate   2. face   3. stab   4. appear
5. misrepresent   6. undermine   7. emerge
8. comment   9. be based on   10. portray   11. lead
12. aim   13. hang around   14. represent / portray

12 Word puzzle

1. forward   2. wonder   3. motivate   4. chorus
5. period   6. bullet   7. lately   8. vision   9. innocent
10. lack   11. on the block; *Vorschlag:* The area around your home, your neighborhood.

13 Word circle

1. pensioner   2. represent   3. turnout   4. though
5. honour   6. replacements   7. stereotype
8. executives   9. sniper

Topic 3

1 Opposites
1. low 2. complicated 3. crowded 4. latest
5. ally 6. to survive

2 New words
1. network; Netzwerk 2. formerly; früher, ehemals
3. software; Software 4. textiles; Textilien, Textilware
5. superpower; Supermacht 6. income; Einkommen
7. clothing; Kleidung 8. rickshaw; Riksha
9. subtitle; Untertitel 10. highlight; Highlight, Höhepunkt 11. necklace; Halskette 12. engineering; Ingenieurwissenschaft, Technik 13. environmentalist; Umweltschützer / -in 14. to outsource; outsourcen
15. backpacker; Rucksacktourist / -in 16. latest; neueste / -r / -s

3 Word families
1. clothing 2. arrival 3. crowded 4. religious
5. taste 6. peaceful 7. independence
8. environmentalist 9. belief

4 Definitions
Vorschlag: 1. The rupee is the currency in India.
2. 'Spaghetti bolognaise', 'curry' and 'fish and chips' are all special dishes. 3. Men usually wear a tie to an interview. They wear it round their neck over a shirt.

5 Matching verbs
1. f) 2. d) 3. a) 4. h) 5. b) 6. g) 7. e) 8. c)

6 Word lines
a) 1. bracelet 2. tie, sari, kurta, salwar kameez
   3. rupee 4. ox
b) 1. vegetarian, Christian 2. selection, location
   3. arrival, rural 4. formerly, hardly

7 Which word?
1. taste 2. cotton 3. prayers 4. densely
5. matter 6. reserve 7. bracelet 8. fairy tale

8 The letter 'o'
[ɒ]: ox, software, hot, cost
[ə]: major, religious, compartment, economy
[ɔː]: formerly, port, to afford, Portuguese
[əʊ]: clothing, location, soldier, low

9 Lost vowels
1. press 2. common 3. value 4. storyline 5. star
6. kidnap 7. research 8. emotional 9. masala
10. recent   *Verstecktes Wort:* politician

10 What am I?
APPEAR

11 What is it?
1. ring 2. husband 3. wedding 4. pyjamas
5. catalogue 6. tight 7. profit 8. wide 9. waistline
10. ankle

12 Almost the same!
1. tourism 2. central 3. expert 4. optimistic
5. wildcat 6. species 7. to locate 8. vehicle

13 First letters
R: reach, ritual, rate   E: expert, endangered
A: alarm, approach   C: central, core, cub, corridor
H: hunt

14 Word puzzle
→: 2. struggle 15. fur 6. emperor 8. dawn
12. outfit 7. marble 9. review 1. exception
11. selection
↓: 3. average 13. hot 14. port 5. arrival
10. fashion 4. economy

Topic 4

1 Definitions

Vorschlag: 1. A disease is an illness, for example, anorexia.   2. When you are seriously ill, you might have to go to hospital and have an operation.
3. When bread has mould on it, it has green and white parts and you shouldn't eat it.   4. If there is very little milk in the refrigerator, you can also say that there is hardly any milk.   5. Drinks that contain a high amount of alcohol are called spirits.   6. If more and more people buy our products, it will definitely lead to a rise in sales.

2 New expressions

1. lunchbox   2. anorexia nervosa   3. wheelchair
4. sixth form   5. self-employment   6. eating disorder

3 One word – two meanings

1. Tisch, Tabelle   2. Botschaft, Nachricht   3. sofort, gerade

4 Wordbuilding

1. decision   2. difficulty   3. to manage to (do s.th.)
4. marriage   5. married   6. criminal   7. rise
8. to impress   9. illness

5 Matching verbs

1. d)   2. g)   3. a)   4. b)   5. f)   6. c)   7. h)   8. e)

6 Word lines

a) 1. lunchbox   2. male   3. vet   4. such as
b) *Vorschläge:* 1. decision, operation   2. mental, physical, illegal   3. agriculture, horticulture
4. homeless, illness

7 Sounds

1. record   2. specific   3. specialist   4. kindergarten
5. study   6. operation   7. common   8. slimmer
9. male   10. consent

8 Which word?

1. agriculture   2. spirits   3. decisions   4. marriage
5. compulsory   6. mould   7. vet   8. nightdress

9 Word puzzle

→: slightly, paintstained, blanket, entity, shiny, chorus, alarmed, friendship

↓: panty, stuck, fanclub, pour, till, fancy, stick, shine, dawn, infinity, nightdress, distance, delight, deal

Lösungswort: Robyn Rihanna Fenty

10 Verbs, verbs, verbs

1. to be dying to do s.th.   2. to beat   3. to keep
4. to creep up   5. to consist of   6. to lie
7. to cuddle   8. to diagnose s.th.   9. to deny
10. to discharge s.o.   11. to recover   12. to turn to s.th. / s.o.   13. to lead

11 First letters

S: sales, sector, to service, to supply
A: automotive, after-sales service, assessment
L: leasing, loan
E: electric, employee, to employ, excellent
S: sales, sector, to service, to supply
F: finance, fashion, financial, flexible, fictional
O: organizational
R: rental, repair
C: chief executive officer (CEO)
E: electric, employee, to employ, excellent

12 Almost the same!

1. financial   2. electric   3. organizational   4. repair

13 What do you say?

1. I think I'm creative.   2. I don't like computers and offices.   3. I don't like working outside in bad weather.   4. I prefer to work with my hands.
5. I'm good with animals.   6. I'm not so good with my hands.   7. I don't find it easy to meet new people.

Puzzles

1 Cryptogram

1	2	3	4	5	6	7	8	9	10
E	N	S	O	R	G	L	Y	W	H
11	12	13	14	15	16	17	18	19	20
I	P	K	C	A	B	D	T	U	V

Topic 1: English is spoken everywhere.
Topic 2: Change we can believe in.
Topic 3: Hollywood or Bollywood?
Topic 4: It isn't easy growing up!

2 Irregular verbs
1. spread, spread 2. lay, lain 3. led, led 4. shone, shone